Crystaline Reiki

A New Frequency Of Healing

Charles Lightwalker

Charles Lightwalker

Dedication

This book is dedicated to the Reiki Masters who came before me, whose efforts paved the way for Reiki to become a recognized and respected healing modality worldwide. Their commitment to providing healing and comfort to those seeking wholeness is truly inspiring.

I would like to extend my heartfelt gratitude to two individuals who have played a significant role in the creation of this book. First, I want to express my deep appreciation to Serena Lasol, a Reiki Master teacher, for her unwavering support and encouragement throughout this journey. Her guidance has been invaluable.

I would also like to extend my thanks to Eric Cunningham, Ph.D., a Reiki Master teacher, for his exceptional editing skills and insightful contributions. His expertise has greatly enhanced the quality and clarity of this work.

Furthermore, I want to acknowledge Dr. Charles Edwards, my dedicated apprentice, for his valuable contribution in writing the Preface (foreword) for this edition of the book. His commitment to upholding the principles of Reiki has been commendable.

In conclusion, I would like to express my gratitude to all those who have supported and believed in me throughout this endeavor. Your unwavering faith and encouragement have been instrumental in bringing this book to fruition.

Charles Lightwalker

Summer 2023, Scotland

Acknowledgment

I would like to express my sincere appreciation to the multitude of students I have had the privilege to teach in both the United States and the United Kingdom. Their unwavering support and encouragement have been instrumental in the creation of this book.

I am particularly grateful to Dr. Joe Crain for granting me permission to incorporate the concept of the gate of grace into my healing practices, specifically in the realm of Crystalline Reiki. This invaluable addition has transformed it into a profoundly effective tool for healing, allowing my clients to experience profound relaxation, rejuvenation, and overall well-being.

The invaluable contributions of esteemed individuals in the field of Reiki and holistic healing have significantly enriched this book. I extend my heartfelt thanks to Reiki Master Teacher, Nichole Andreasen, Healing Light Teacher and cherished friend, Dr. Meg Blackburn-Losey, and my closest confidant, Dr. Pat Dougherty D.C., with whom I coauthored the book Quantum Healing: The Synergy of Chiropractic and Reiki. I am also deeply grateful for the insightful contributions of Dr. Rita Louise, a respected Medical Intuitive Teacher, and longtime friend, as well as Dr. Amina Kazeem Olawale from Nigeria, and lastly, but certainly not least, my beloved daughter River.

Without the wisdom, expertise, and support of these remarkable individuals and the countless students who have touched my life, this book would not have been possible. I am truly humbled and indebted to each and every one of them for their unwavering support and profound influence on my journey.

Table of Contents

About the Author

Charles is a seasoned practitioner with over thirty-five years of experience in the field of complementary care and holistic healing. With a strong background in religious studies, he holds a doctorate in the subject and has served as a minister, chaplain, religious counselor, and medical intuitive. Charles's extensive knowledge and expertise have been further honed through his work with shamans, master healers, and various complementary care practitioners. Over the past twenty-five years, he has dedicated himself to the practice of Reiki and has become highly proficient in this healing modality.

In addition to Reiki, Charles also specializes in sound healing with tuning forks, the Metis Medicine ways, intuitive healing arts, and the operation of holistic enterprises. His comprehensive skill set has made him an exceptional instructor, as he imparts his wisdom through teaching Reiki, sound healing, medical intuition, and the Metis Medicine Ways. Furthermore, Charles is a sought-after speaker, captivating audiences with his enlightening lectures on holistic healing, medical intuition, spiritual living, new thought beliefs, and metaphysical subjects.

Outside of his professional endeavors, Charles finds solace in activities that promote inner peace and self-care. He enjoys walking, hiking, practicing yoga, meditation, and writing. Living in the picturesque surroundings of Scotland, he often finds tranquility by strolling along the beach with his partner Serena and their daughter River. Charles's personal journey of healing, sparked by his own experiences of injuries and trauma during his time in the Army, has guided his commitment to helping others find their path to wellness and self-discovery. By delving into the core of trauma, injuries, and illnesses, he believes true healing can be achieved, and he continues to inspire and guide individuals on this transformative journey.

https://charleslightwalker9.wixsite.com/charleslightwalker

Foreword

Welcome to Crystaline Reiki. The information in this book comes from Charles Lightwalker's life-long spiritual journey as a Reiki Healer. The thoughts, ideas, and methods described here have been evolving and expanding for over thirty years.

Charles is a Usui Reiki Master. He studied Crystal Reiki under the Star of David with crystals, and Sacred Flames Reiki, where gazing at the flame grounds you before you begin the Reiki Session. In 2000 Charles became a Gathered Master through G. W. Hardin and Joseph Crane. The life-changing experience at his Gathering refined his knowledge of the Gate of Grace Sacred Healing Space.

Charles' work in using healing energies, sound healing with tuning forks, shamanic and spiritual healing methods, and divine guidance are combined in this new frequency of healing called "Crystaline Reiki."

Charles is Métis (meaning mixed-blood) and was born to parents of both French-Scottish, and Native American heritage. Growing up in the "white man's world," it was not until he had reached his late twenties that he was told that his great grandfather was a Cherokee warrior. This was the beginning of his search to discover and understand a culture that was foreign to him.

Studying with shamans and medicine women, Charles began using his natural ability to see through the veils of illusion, to understand the healing ways of energy, rocks, and crystals. He responded to his inner calling and began to use these abilities to be of service to humankind.

Crystaline Reiki with shamanic healing assists the healing process and stimulates wellness, vitality, balance, and peace. Crystaline Reiki and shamanic healing are forms of energy healing, ancient and powerful methods of natural healing used today in conjunction with, or as an alternative to, traditional medicine, that restore the balance among the physical, emotional, spiritual, and mental levels of all living beings. At the soul level, they can also effect reconnection among all spiritual beings and the Universe. They are useful in maintaining, as well as restoring balance. You don't have to be suffering from a disease to benefit from it.

Every living being possesses an internal and external energy field. Crystaline Reiki and shamanic healing address the energetic and physical systems by releasing blockages and past wounds and restoring balance, thereby facilitating physical and emotional healing and spiritual growth, allowing you to step fully into who you are becoming. Charles' practice incorporates several complementary modalities:

Crystaline Reiki, other Métis shamanic practices, sound healing, and medical intuition.

You'll experience relief and support for a variety of issues. Some of these include, but are not limited to:

- Acceleration of healing from injuries/illnessess

- Promotion of relaxation and quality of life

- Alleviation from age-related problems

- Boosting immunity• Releasing emotional trauma

- Resolving behavioral issues

- Assistence in detoxification

- Maximization of health before and after surgery

- Making the process of 'death' easier• Promoting of spiritual growth

Shamanic Healing Principles

Service: Charles' practice endeavors to assist people in their healing processes, to aid in accelerating healing, to reduce pain, and to facilitate rebalancing. In Métis shamanism, healers are considered to be of service to the community.

Integrity: The truth is not always pleasant; sometimes we are mirrors to people. The trick is to reflect without repelling; to be honest without causing pain.

Balance: The heart of Charles' work is restoration of balance. That which is blocked is unblocked (tracking and releasing energy), that which is missing is returned (soul retrieval), and that which does not belong is extracted; all with permission, in harmony, and in accordance with the client's will/intent.

Accountability: Each of us is accountable and responsible for our actions, and ourselves. Without accountability, there cannot be healing. The healer is only the facilitator; the client drives the session.

Love: Universal love is one of the Saywas or Seven Organizing Principles in Peruvian shamanism, and it is the journey of the Medicine Person to master them. These are not intellectual concepts, but essential ways of knowing. "Love" makes the impossible possible.

Additional Modalities

Charles has continued his studies in alternative healing methods, such as:

- Reiki
- Vibrational Medicine
- Stone Medicine
- Spiritual Healing
- Yoga
- Kinesiology
- Sound Healing
- Medical Intuition
- Shamanic Healing

- Color Therapy
- Dance Therapy
- Vibrational Yoga Therapy
- Kryahgenetics
- Soul Journey WorkReflexology

He combines many of these healing modalities into a progressive healing treatment that can have a profound effect in assisting a person on their healing journey.

Professional Organizations

Charles is a member of the following professional organizations:

- International Association of Medical Intuitives
- International Natural Healers Association
- International Holistic Therapies Directory
- Natural Health Resource Alliance Spiritual Healers and Earth Stewards The Metaphysical Research Society
- Complimentary Health Alliance
- Sound Healers of Washington
- Sound Healers Association International Association of Sound Healers
- Vibrational Yoga Alliance
- World Reiki Association
- International Association of Healthcare Practitioner Society of Shamanic Practitioners
- Metis Medicine Society

Introduction

Crystaline Reiki: A New Frequency of Healing

You are about to embark on a new adventure in Reiki Healing. This manual will guide you through the process of Crystaline Reiki. The dynamic frequency of this healing energy has already helped many begin their journey to wellness. If you have studied Reiki and have an understanding of the principals of Chi energy, then you will understand how this increased frequency of energy called 'Crystaline Reiki' will intensify the healing process of the individual being healed. Fixing a healing intention with spirit and angelic guides, sound healing with tuning forks to clear the chakras, in a sacred healing space combined with Reiki, creates this dynamic and powerful healing frequency we call Crystaline Reiki. As you continue reading, keep an open mind and heart.

Chapter One: A Reiki Overview

Reiki Defined

Reiki is a compound Japanese word that connotes the general meaning of "healing." *Rei* means sacred or spiritual. *Ki* means life force energy, the same energy as chi in Chinese, ti in Hawaiian, and super strings in physics. Whatever you call it, ki is the energy that runs through everything. Ki flow is unlimited and anyone can tap in to it for healing. Most Westerners take Reiki to mean "universal life force energy." This universal energy, and not personal energy, is what is used during Reiki healing. The Usui Natural Healing System (sometimes written as Usui Shiki Ryoho), named after its founder, Mikao Usui, is the basic system used to invoke and use this energy known as Reiki.

Reiki Precepts

Just for today, do not be angry.

Just for today, do not worry and be filled with gratitude.

Just for today, devote yourself to your work and be kind to people.

Every morning and evening, join your hands in prayer.

The Chakras

Chakra is a Sanskrit word meaning "wheel." Chakras are energy centers within the body that turn or rotate as they process the life force energy.

There are eleven energy centers within your body, and an aura field that connects you to the twelfth, the divine energy of Source. These energy centers are connected to the organs, the meridians, and the emotional and thought centers of the body. They keep the life force energy flowing throughout the body. Each chakra is related to a gland or several glands in the physical body. The chakras can therefore be seen as a subtle addition to the glandular system. Healing the relevant chakra helps glandular functions. Keeping the chakras in balance is an important key to good health.

The Traditional Reiki Degrees

All Reiki derives from the Usui Natural Healing System, more commonly known as traditional Usui Reiki. In traditional Usui Reiki a student goes through a comprehensive many-year-long learning program to earn Reiki I, Reiki II, and then Reiki Master degrees.

Traditional Reiki I—the first degree. This is the first of the Reiki degrees, where students learn how to do self-treatment and to give hands-on treatment to others. Many, particularly people with chronic problems, take the First Degree Reiki training to help with their own personal healing. In this degree a Reiki Teaching Master gives several initiations. These initiations "attune" each student to open the Reiki energy channels and ensure that energy passed through will not be from the person's own reserves. Students are given a series of exercises that they must do after the class for at least three weeks to make attunements permanent and available from then on as needed. This level generally requires two and a half days of training. Many ctraditional Teaching Reiki Masters provide this training in an eight to ten-hour class with quite a bit of homework. In class the student learns a little of the Reiki history and the simple basic skills to use Reiki. They have an opportunity to work with a Teaching Reiki Master to learn basic hands-on healing, grounding, and protection. The student will then continue to work with their Teaching Reiki Master for a few months to refine their skills and technique.

Traditional Reiki II—the second degree. Second level training is usually given only after a student has been practicing first-degree skills for at least a year, though this can vary somewhat depending on the individual. This second level generally requires two days of training that many current Teaching Reiki Masters teach as an eight-hour class, plus significant homework. The second degree Reiki student learns three special symbols and how to use these symbols to improve their focus and increase the amounts of Reiki energy transferred. The three symbols loosely represent the trinity present in many belief systems. In this case, representing mind, body, and spirit, with one symbol for each concept. Second Degree Reiki also teaches students how to give distance treatments for individuals, groups, and circumstances. It provides tools to help with emotional and mental problems, physical complaints, past-life and karmic issues, and how to direct healing energy both forward and backward in time and space, including over great distances. Students who are ready can learn second-degree skills over the weekend.

Traditional Reiki Master—the third degree. Traditional Teaching Reiki Master training is primarily intended for people who have made Reiki their life's work. The requirements for the second Reiki degree are stringent. They are even more stringent and difficult for a Reiki Master degree. Depending upon the individual, Reiki Master level training is usually only given after a student has been practicing second-degree skills for at least two years. After being accepted by Q-Teaching Reiki Master as an apprentice, it takes from one to three additional years of hands-on training and experience to master teaching each of the three levels of training. During this training period as a courtesy, the student is called a Reiki Master. Soon after starting their Reiki Master Program, they gain the knowledge to be a Reiki teacher. Still, they have a long way to go to add the considerable hands-on experience under the careful guidance of a good teacher to become an effective teacher.

During this apprenticeship phase, each new Reiki Master is strongly encouraged to heal others and themselves, helping each to improve their own physical, spiritual, and mental health.

A New Frequency of Healing

Put the energy of traditional Reiki together with wisdom, and the Gate of Grace, and you have the most powerful, yet gentle source of healing energy available today: Crystaline Reiki.

Because Crystaline Reiki is from Prime Source, God, Goddess, Buddha, Great Spirit, or whatever name you may wish to use, you or anyone else can use it. We are all equal and we all have the ability to heal others and ourselves. All that is needed to channel Crystaline Reiki energy is an open mind, an open heart, and the desire and intention to heal. I have been asked the question: "Aren't all the different types of Reiki just Reiki?"

I like to think that these "schools" of Reiki are expressions of various qualities of color/light frequencies that have come via the Reiki frequency stream. In effect, they are all Reiki at their core. As we co-create our lives with spirit/source, we express our individuality and creativity by the way we experience, teach, and practice healing.

Instead of considering one form of Reiki frequency over another, we might consider simply honoring this creative expression, and understand that diversity in frequency will better respond to the needs of many people.

You, like me, were likely drawn to certain forms of healing. Sometimes it is just your intuition or spirit guides leading you to this healing modality. I know that it was no mistake that I was given the vision of Crystaline Reiki. Crystaline Reiki is a school of Reiki that includes symbols of Usui and Tibetan, as well as channeled information. There are five practitioner symbols.

The first practitioner level uses no symbol and is simply attuning the person to universal life force energy, whereas the second level uses four symbols. In the master level, the Crystaline Reiki symbol is employed. In addition to using these symbols, creating a sacred space, aligning the chakras with tuning forks, setting the intention, connecting with your spirit guides, and letting go of the outcome makes Crystaline Reiki a powerful modality for healing.

The sounds and combinations of sounds from the tuning forks are unique to every healing session. Surrounding the client inside a sacred space allows the client to fully open to their own healing vibrations, thus, allowing healing to take place on all levels of their being.

Crystaline Reiki is taught to those who are already healers, Reiki Masters, sound therapists, and massage therapists. Some may say this is not fair, but experience has shown me that a person must be ready to experience this shift in vibration that is Crystaline Reiki.

Chapter Two: Crystaline Reiki Questions Answered

Crystaline Reiki is a gentle, non-intrusive form of hands-on healing that falls under the category of complementary and alternative therapies.

The National Institute of Health classifies Reiki as a "biofield energy therapy" and is currently funding studies to measure its effects. Developed in Japan in the late 1800s, Reiki has been practiced in the United States since the 1930s. Scientific-based studies have begun on Reiki, but early evidence shows what Reiki practitioners have always known: Reiki effectively relieves stress, decreases pain, and accelerates healing on mental and emotional as well as physical levels. Studies at the Cross Cancer Research Center in Canada and the University of Michigan support the use of Reiki as an adjunct treatment for acute or chronic pain. At the Portsmouth Regional Hospital in New Hampshire, Reiki is used to ease anxiety in patients preparing for surgery. Reiki is especially useful for reducing stress. The ki in Reiki is a subtle form of the ki or chi found in the martial arts of aikido or tai chi. Applied through gentle touch, Reiki healing stimulates and restores the body's vital energy, thus healing body, heart, and mind.

Why Crystaline Reiki?

Eastern philosophies say there are two major life force energies. One kind of energy is that of personal/individual life energy. When it is used up, that living thing dies. There are ways to tap into this individual energy, but in doing so even the most vital healers rapidly tire and become depleted. Tapping this type of energy is unhealthy. Reiki energy provides a far better alternative. Reiki energy is universal life force energy. It is inexhaustible, plus is intelligent. It always goes to where it will do the most good and never comes in stronger than can be handled. Crystaline Reiki provides a simple, easy to learn way to tap in to this universal energy to help others and ourselves.

What is the Definition of 'Crystaline'?

Crystaline is the word for amplified energy. A Crystaline Reiki practitioner uses a higher vibrational frequency in the healing process. Combined with Reiki it is a higher frequency of healing energy.

What Does Crystaline Reiki Do?

Crystaline Reiki is not a substitute for appropriate medical or emotional treatment. Reiki is a complementary treatment, and should be used only as an adjunct when other forms of treatment are necessary. Reiki is a very gentle and safe method of bringing in healing energy from the Universal supply. Reiki uses ancient healing energy techniques to help build more personal energy, more vitality, more resilience, and better health. Its most profound effect is an almost immediate feeling of deep relaxation, resulting in a reduction in stress. Reiki can help you change your mind and body for the better by learning more of your inner self and giving more to yourself. You can learn to share Reiki healing energy with others as well as anything else that you can imagine, including pets and plants! There are many cases on record of miraculous cures where Reiki has helped with all kinds of physical and mental ailments. Reiki practitioners can even send Reiki over a distance, sometimes thousands of miles, and still achieve beneficial effects. Reiki is being used more and more as an adjunct to help with traditional medical practices.

What Does Crystaline Reiki Energy Feel Like?

People feel Crystaline Reiki in different ways. Most often during treatment, the energy is experienced as warmth. Others feel a mild tingle, as when an arm or leg has fallen asleep. Still others feel a throbbing or pulsing sensation. Some people don't feel any physical sensation but describe mental or emotional changes, such as a sense of calmness or peacefulness. Nearly everyone experiences a Reiki treatment as "deeply relaxing."

When is a Crystaline Reiki Treatment Appropriate?

Crystaline Reiki is particularly effective if applied as soon as possible after trauma happens, whether due to physical injury, or mental shock. At these times the body is mobilizing all available energy to stabilize the immediate problem so that long-term healing can occur. Any extra energy available will only enhance the process.

Later, when the healing process slows and energy is shared between healing and other bodily functions and activities, Reiki can still be a useful adjunct. It is important to remember that because Crystaline Reiki works on any energy level, it can aid physical, emotional, mental, and even spiritual healing.

Many people also use Crystaline Reiki as a preventive practice. Practitioners learn to do self-treatment before they learn how to treat others. Many of us are increasingly aware of the unique energy patterns that develop between individuals and among people in groups. Psychology defines this with the term "group dynamics." Advanced Reiki practitioners are trained to treat group situations as well, using special distance techniques.

What is a Crystaline Reiki Treatment?

A Crystaline Reiki treatment is a "laying on of hands," an ancient technique common to many spiritual traditions. To ensure the safety of the client as well as the practitioner, only a person fully trained and certified in Crystaline Reiki techniques should administer Crystaline Reiki treatments.

In a typical Crystaline Reiki treatment, the client lies down (fully clothed) on a padded treatment table. Energy is transferred to the client through the hands of the practitioner. The practitioner moves through a sequence of standard hand positions. Treatment starts

with the practitioner's hands lightly resting on or above the client's head for three to five minutes, followed by slow and systematic similar hand positions, down the body to the feet. The patient almost always feels the energy begin to flow into them, either as heat or a strange flow through their body; often in places remote from the point at which the practitioner has their hands.

A full treatment usually takes about an hour. A Crystaline Reiki treatment is a spiritual practice because it works directly with energy, or "spirit." This type of treatment does not involve any pressure or manipulation of tissues, such as with a massage.

How Does a Crystaline Reiki Treatment Work?

This question is best answered by drawing an analogy. As mentioned before, our natural energy level is affected by our state of health or disease. We can all relate to the feelings of low energy or depletion that occur when we are trying to heal, whether from physical distress (illness or injury) or from mental difficulties (such as grief or anxiety). A Reiki treatment under these circumstances can be compared to jump-starting a car. When the car's battery can't quite provide enough energy to start the car, we attach jumper cables from another battery to add more energy.

Reiki is a means of adding more energy to our life force battery to help jump-start the healing process. This process does not exhaust the practitioner, who is trained to channel energy from the outside environment, not from his or her own personal "battery." Practiced in this manner, the energy available is virtually limitless. The amount of energy transferred depends on the client's ability to use it and willingness to receive it. When no more energy can the transfer ceases to occur. A skillful practitioner can usually sense when this happens.

Does Crystaline Reiki Work For Everyone?

Crystaline Reiki works to the degree that a person is willing to use the energy. If a person chooses, for whatever reason, to be closed, and not receive a treatment, no energy will be transferred. The effects of a Crystaline Reiki treatment can be so subtle it may not even be felt. The healthier you are, the more subtle the effects.

Most of us feel some discomfort in our lives and can benefit from Reiki.

Crystaline Reiki is known as intelligent energy and helps with the highest form of healing possible in a situation. Sometimes the healing that occurs may not match our own expectations. This is often where the spiritual aspect of Reiki is most obvious.

If a person's time has come, being able to feel at peace with death is the highest form of healing possible, even though we personally think a complete cure is preferable. Reiki can only enhance whatever natural healing is taking place; it cannot be used to guarantee outcomes or change fate.

Who Can Do Crystaline Reiki?

Because Crystaline Reiki is from Prime Source, God, Goddess, Buddha, Great Spirit, or whatever name you may wish to use, you or anyone else can use it. We are all equal, and we all have the ability to heal others and ourselves. All that is needed to channel Crystaline Reiki Energy is an open mind, an open heart, and the desire and intention to heal.

The Crystaline Reiki Degrees

The Crystaline Reiki degrees offer the practitioner a higher vibration of frequency in the energy matrix that is being used in the healing process. Placing the client in the sacred healing space enhances the healing process of Crystaline Reiki. When looking for a Crystaline Reiki practitioner, take time to discuss their training with them before you commit to receive treatments. As in many other unregulated professions, there are people who prefer to take shortcuts in their training rather than invest the time and money to become fully skilled. Crystaline Reiki training changes a person's life. Whenever a Crystaline Reiki practitioner gives a treatment, they are receiving Crystaline Reiki energy themselves and their own healing processes are stimulated.

That means any personal issues that require healing will be brought to the surface more quickly than they were before. I have seen some pretty incredible explosive releases on the part of both Crystaline Reiki students and Crystaline Reiki Masters during Crystaline Reiki treatments.

I know that during such a release I want to be in the company of someone I trust, who is very nurturing, and who would be able to do the right things in an emergency. If training and the accompanying initiations are taken too quickly, the challenges for growth can be unsettling, to say the least. You will be much happier if you carefully chose qualified experienced Crystaline Reiki practitioners and teachers.

Chapter Three: The Healing Power of Crystaline Reiki

Reiki translates from the Japanese to universal life force energy. Crystaline means to increase the frequency of energy. Today the word stands for a system of healing and self-empowerment popular all over the world. Ki is the name of life energy in Japan. Other cultures with ancient roots in the metaphysical have similar words for this force. In China, it's called Chi. The discipline of t'ai chi works with this energy. The Hindu traditions, from yoga to Ayurveda (Indian natural medicine), call it prana. The Hawaiian kahunas, or medicine men, called it mana. It is the animating spirit of all living things. Star Wars fans in our modern pop culture might now call it the force. They are all similar concepts for life energy. Usually, through touching another, a Crystaline Reiki practitioner channels this life force for the recipient's healing. The recipient's body draws in the energy as if sucking a straw. The practitioner is like the straw: they are only the channeler. The source of this energy is the limitless supply of life force in the universe. The energy is used to stimulate their healing systems, used by the body to go where it most needs. The immune system is activated and bolstered. Cells receive more power to heal wounds and defend the body from parasites. Crystaline Reiki quickens the detoxification of the body of all poisons. Crystaline Reiki also works on levels other than the physical. It works on the recipient's emotional, mental, and spiritual components to get to the root of the problem. Although everyone responds to treatment differently, recipients of this healing energy report they are calmer, less stressed, and generally feel better. Some relax, while others feel energized.

Crystaline Reiki differs from other forms of energy healing, such as therapeutic touch or spiritual healing, because the recipient is in control.

They can never "overdose" on energy because once they have enough, the process unconsciously stops. Crystaline Reiki is safe and gentle. The practitioner is not using his own energy and thus does not get tired or feel like he is taking on the client's ailments. Crystaline Reiki practitioners' hands get hot when working, and recipients report increased warmth or tingling during a session. The practitioner will hold various hand positions on the body while the recipient lies on a table. No massage or manipulation of tissue is involved. Crystaline Reiki is strictly a spiritual energy process, although some massage therapists also do Crystaline Reiki. Once you are trained in Crystaline Reiki, simple thought triggers the energy, so massage therapists who do Crystaline Reiki are always channeling some energy if the recipient needs it.

Crystaline Reiki really does work on all levels, wherever it is needed most. Although this is not common, I have had clients who spontaneously experience memories from the past with vividness during sessions. Most are traumatic memories from childhood or other stressful times. They had felt resolved on the issue but had really never dealt with it. Others rekindle pleasant memories of love, friendship, and happiness. Crystaline Reiki is working on healing the emotional nature and releasing or triggering what they need for their highest good. I've found not only is the recipient's body in charge of the energy transfer, but their highest aspect, their unconscious, super conscious, higher self (or whatever word you choose to use) is the one truly in charge.

During a Crystaline Reiki course, the Crystaline Reiki master teacher attunes you to the energy through a simple ceremony, most often involving symbols of healing, creating sacred space, balancing the chakras, and breathing. A Crystaline Reiki master teacher is simply one who can teach Crystaline Reiki. Mere teaching is involved. Most fill their classes with history, theory, and practice time to occupy the rational side of the brain, but once you have the Crystaline Reiki attunement, you can immediately and easily channel the energy for the rest of your life. The Crystaline Reiki teacher holds this special frequency, and as if you are a radio receiver, he tunes you to the frequency of pure energy. The attunement simply aligns your personal energy to be a channel for Crystaline Reiki. One who has not had an attunement from someone who has this energy is not doing Crystaline Reiki. Many very similar forms of healing can be just as effective in different ways, and these techniques are often confused with Crystaline Reiki.

Once you are attuned to Crystaline Reiki, the benefits are enormous. You have access to healing energy at any time. Touch is your vehicle of healing for yourself and others. While driving to work, or stuck in a traffic jam, place one hand on your leg. The Crystaline Reiki starts flowing. Do Crystaline Reiki while watching TV or when on the phone. Maintain your health in this hectic world. When feeling stressed, angry, or depressed, use Crystaline Reiki to feel better. If you have a headache, or any other aches or pains, Crystaline Reiki them away. This healing technique is not a substitute for conventional medicine, but it supports recovery and accelerates healing.

Many hospitals now have some form of Reiki available pre- and post-operation. Chiropractors and other healthcare facilitators are looking into the benefits of Crystaline Reiki. You don't have to decide to be a healer and give up your day job to do Crystaline Reiki. Most Crystaline Reiki practitioners are not nurses, doctors, massage therapists, chiropractors, or healers. Many are drawn to the healing arts after Crystaline Reiki. Still, the vast amount of Crystaline Reiki practitioners out there is ordinary people with ordinary jobs, from executives to homemakers and everything in between. The first and only person you are truly responsible for healing on all levels is yourself. Crystaline Reiki helps you accomplish this. If you can aid others on the way, that is a beautiful gift, but ultimately they are healing themselves. You are only providing a boost of energy.

The benefits of Crystaline Reiki

Basically, Crystaline Reiki is meant for the personal growth of the individual who receives an attunement, which includes physical, emotional, mental, and spiritual spheres. Once a person is attuned and gives him- or herself regular treatment, Crystaline Reiki works its way, automatically making positive changes in his/her physical, emotional, mental, and spiritual states. Consciously, he/she may use it for any positive purpose to which his/her intuition guides.

Here are a few of the uses/benefits:

*Crystaline Reiki relaxes the body and mind and releases tension. Thus it makes a person more balanced and peaceful. It Helps in clearing anxiety, depression, and phobias. Daily self-treatment can keep the person in maximum health and well-being.

*Bless your food, drinks, and medicines with Crystaline Reiki to increase their vibration. Giving Crystaline Reiki to medicines before use can minimize their harmful side effects.

*When a loved one is sick, your gift of a Crystaline Reiki healing session will help him/her recover earlier.

*Send treatment to a family member or a friend who lives a distance away. This requires Second Degree Crystaline Reiki.

*Use Crystaline Reiki symbols for meditation to increase your spiritual abilities and to increase the vibration of love and healing in your home. This also requires at least Crystaline Reiki Second Degree. Use Crystaline Reiki to improve your relationships. Although not a medical system, Crystaline Reiki can treat virtually all known ailments. At the physical level, it can heal all types of pain and treat acute as well as chronic diseases. Crystaline Reiki is known to have cured hypertension, cancer, heart diseases, and arthritis, in addition to many of the less serious ailments. However, in some instances, it may be advisable to get regular medical treatment and use Crystaline Reiki to support that for better and quicker results.

*Crystaline Reiki is excellent for treating complicated diseases, particularly where the disease's cause is unknown.

*Chronically ill patients can use Crystaline Reiki to restore lost energy due to more invasive treatment (i.e., chemotherapy, radiation, and surgery). It can be used to lessen pain, enhance the immune system, and lower stress-related anxiety about the illness.

*Crystaline Reiki energy basically has five effects: It brings about deep relaxation; dissolves energy blockages and vitalizes chakra centers; detoxifies; supplies healing; Universal life-force energy; and increases the vibrational frequency of the body.

*It adjusts according to the needs of the recipient, supports the body's natural healing abilities, and balances the body's energies. There is no overdoing in Crystaline Reiki.

*It improves mental well-being and gradually cleanses the body's toxins (poisons).

*It helps people break bad habits. For those people who are not apparently ill, a series of Crystaline Reiki treatment sessions makes them more confident and balanced by making positive changes in their attitude and lifestyle. Crystaline Reiki can thus bring them a happier and healthier life.

*It creates decency in general behavior and makes a person more thoughtful.

*Applying Crystaline Reiki to the workplace can create a congenial atmosphere and improve working efficiency.

*Crystaline Reiki can treat even those who are not physically present with us. This energy is not bound by time and distance and can be sent to anyone, no matter where the person may be living. This requires attunements for Crystaline Reiki Second Degree.

*Since the energy flows through the practitioner while giving a Crystaline Reiki treatment, the practitioner automatically receives healing.

*Crystaline Reiki can be effectively used to treat plants and animals also. It considerably improves their growth and health. When given Crystaline Reiki, they enjoy the energy and express the joy in their own way.

*Practically, you can give Crystaline Reiki to anything, be it living, non-living, a machine, a situation, or a relationship. The use of Crystaline Reiki is wider than what has been suggested above. If you can perceive what Crystaline Reiki is, you can use it for much more without having to look for a list of its uses. Our lack of ingenuity or imagination does not limit the energy and its uses.

*Crystaline Reiki as a preventive medicine. Eastern medical philosophy has always emphasized the superiority of maintaining good health over curing illness. Crystaline Reiki is a preventive medicine par excellence. But it is even more: when practicing Crystaline Reiki on yourself or others, you experience both its preventive and curative functions simultaneously. If you have a disease, Crystaline Reiki will cure it; if not, Crystaline Reiki will promote your health and longevity. This preventive cum curative quality of Reiki makes it a unique healing system.It is natural to be healthy. When certain parts of our bodies fail to function naturally, sickness occurs. The causes may be bacteria and viruses, organic (toxins), or psychosomatic. Bacteria and viruses are always present in our bodies. Still, they are kept in check (sometimes even exploited to do useful work for us) as long as our bodies function naturally. Toxins are continually clogging our organs, but as long as we function naturally, the chemicals produced by our body will neutralize these toxins.

Our brain is continually stressed, but if nature runs its course, we will be adequately relieved after sleep and rest. The Eastern concept of health is also wider than that of the West. To be healthy is not just to be free from disease. A person cannot be called healthy if they are often restless, irritable, or forgetful, cannot concentrate or sleep soundly, and have no zest for work or play.

How Crystaline Reiki promotes health

First, it frees us from disease; it prevents and cures illness. Then it helps us to grow emotionally, mentally, and spiritually, giving us the incredible benefits of health in its broader sense. The preventive and curative qualities of Crystaline Reiki can be reduced to two simple principles: the cleansing of meridians and the balancing of the chakras to achieve a harmonious energy flow.

How Crystaline Reiki prevents or cures contagious diseases

When disease-causing microorganisms attack certain parts of the body, reserve energy is channeled to meet these attacks. But if the meridians are blocked, the flow of reserve energy is hindered, and illness results. When using Crystaline Reiki, you cleanse the meridians, harmonizing energy levels, and promote a smooth flow of reserve energy to the areas under attack, thus restoring balance. Practicing Crystaline Reiki increases our reserves of energy, thus preventing any possible future outbreak of illness.

Chapter Four: Learn Crystaline Reiki

Crystaline Reiki is probably the simplest and easiest holistic healing method available to us, so anyone can learn to use Crystaline Reiki, whatever their age or gender, religion or origin. No specific knowledge or experience is required—only a desire to learn, a willingness to allow this healing energy to flow through you, and a little time to attend your first course and to practice the skills you learn.

The ability to channel Crystaline Reiki can only be acquired by being transferred to the student by a Crystaline Reiki master teacher during the special attunement process that is part of a Crystaline Reiki workshop. This attunement process makes Crystaline Reiki unique and is the reason why the ability to heal can be developed so quickly yet so permanently. The attunement reactivates a Crystaline Reiki channel within your energy field through which the Crystaline Reiki can flow. Once you have been attuned, you will be able to use Crystaline Reiki for the rest of your life—the ability to channel Crystaline Reiki does not wear off or wear out! From then on, whenever you intend to use Crystaline Reiki, simply thinking about it or holding your hands out in readiness to use it will activate it. There are no complicated rituals to follow. There are four levels of training, often referred to as "degrees,"—but these do not refer to any academic level or qualification!

First degree

You usually receive four "attunements," which gradually open up your inner healing channel, allowing Crystaline Reiki to flow through you. The emphasis at this level is on self-healing, although you will also be taught how to treat family and friends and how to use Crystaline Reiki with animals and plants.

Second degree

This course is suitable for people who have already had several months of experience using Crystaline Reiki on themselves and/or others and want to become Crystaline Reiki Practitioners or wish to use the additional skills for their own personal growth and spiritual development. It includes another one or two attunements which enable you to access even more Crystaline Reiki, and you learn three sacred symbols and their sacred names and some special ways of using them, including a form of distant healing that enables you to send a Crystaline Reiki treatment to anyone, anywhere, at any time, with the same effectiveness as if that person was with you.

Third degree

This is the level of a Crystaline Reiki master, which is essentially making a life-long commitment to the mastery of Crystaline Reiki.

Fourth degree

This is the level a person reaches when they have attained an attunement to teach Crystaline Reiki and is a Crystaline Reiki master teacher. They then help spread the teachings of Crystaline Reiki to the world, helping to spread healing to all who ask. What is a Crystaline Reiki attunement? Crystaline Reiki practitioners are said to be "attuned" to the Crystaline Reiki energy. The attunement is similar to helping someone tune in to a radio station, but in the case of Crystaline Reiki, it allows the student to tune in more efficiently and use Crystaline Reiki energy. Everyone is, to some degree, attuned to the same energies used within Crystaline Reiki. Teaching Crystaline Reiki Masters give initiations to better connect each student with the energy channels and to ensure that energy passed through will not be from the student's own reserves. Teaching Crystaline Reiki Masters go through considerable training to learn how to make efficient attunements and impart the Crystaline Reiki teachings. After each attunement, students are given a series of exercises for twenty-one days or longer to ensure those students are, from then on, permanently attached to the Crystaline Reiki energy they learn.

Attunements

Attunements are a part of what separates Crystaline Reiki and Usui Reiki from other energy modalities. We all have the ability to connect to the source, which is life force energy. When we are first born, we are totally connected to it. As we begin to grow and become more aware of our physical and emotional bodies, with the thoughts and sensations that accompany this three-dimensional reality, our connection to source gets weaker. Attunements are a powerful way to re-establish our connection to that source. During an attunement process, it is not uncommon to experience light-headedness or visions or to perspire heavily. Frequently, individuals will have emotional releases and experience a strong sense of being cleansed in spirit, soul, and body. Many people experience a cleansing period later. During junk foods. After receiving the attunement, sometimes up to thirty days this time, it is best to stay away from alcohol and smoking and make sure that you get plenty of rest. Saunas or sweats during this time can be beneficial. Be sure and drink lots of water; it assists in flushing toxins from your body. Vibrational yoga-focusing methods are a good source of help during this period. Get a six-by-eight-inch card, and on one side, write out your intentions. On the other side, draw a symbol that represents this intention to you. Light a favorite candle and set this card behind it, with the symbol facing forward. While focusing your eyes on the candle, your subconscious mind will see the symbol, even though your natural mind will not. This simple procedure will balance both hemispheres of your brain and improve your powers of concentration. Do this for five minutes the first time, ten minutes the second time, and fifteen minutes the third time. Maintain this fifteen-minute period of focusing on the candle for ten days and then increase that time to twenty minutes. Maintain this twenty-minute period for another ten days, at which time you are free to either increase the time again or leave it at the twenty minutes. Do as your intuition is guiding you to do.

What is a Crystaline Reiki distance treatment?

Only a Crystaline Reiki Level 2 or a Crystaline Reiki Master can give a distance treatment. Crystaline Reiki distance treatments are learned advanced techniques for transferring Reiki energy to a distant time or location. Although we do not understand either the energy or how it works, there is considerable evidence that Reiki is able to travel independent of time or distance to deliver healing. As with the telephone, most Reiki practitioners use this technique knowing that it works and not necessarily having a clue as to the underlying mechanisms.

Group Crystaline Reiki

Group Crystaline Reiki or Shuchu Reiki involves a group of Crystaline Reiki practitioners working together on a single client. This can make for a shorter treatment time, and the intensity of the treatment is increased as more practitioners are involved.

One version of the group treatment familiar in several Western styles of Reiki involves an equal number of practitioners working on each side of the client's body and one working at the head.

While symmetry of treatment is the goal here, it is not absolutely necessary. If there are not enough people to cover all the positions when working on the front or back of the client (especially when using a hand placement set with a large number of positions), then just as in a standard one-person treatment, the practitioners may move on to other positions in succession.

Group Reiki sessions can be quite powerful, especially if using Crystaline Reiki as part of the treatment process. When Crystaline Reiki is used in a group process, it is advisable to have one practitioner balance the chakras with the tuning fork while other practitioners are working on various areas of the body, with one at the head of the person.

Crystaline Reiki with massage

In combining Crystaline Reiki with massage, you create a deeper relaxation of the client, allowing him/her to accept the muscular movement of the therapist's hands in doing deep tissue work.

Crystaline Reiki with reflexology

Crystaline Reiki blended with reflexology continues the progress towards creating a multi-dimensional touch through the body reflex zones. Both hands and feet have reflex points that correlate to all the glands, organs, and other parts of the body. The reflex points you find in your hands will be found in the feet as well. Anything found on the left side of the body, such as your heart, will be found in your left hand or foot. Anything found on the right side of the body, such as the appendix, will be found in your right hand or foot. Stimulating these reflex points properly can help many health problems in a natural way. When Crystaline Reiki is combined with reflexology, massage, sound healing, or spiritual healing, the effectiveness of the healing is enhanced dramatically.

Chapter Five: Crystaline Reiki Certification Explained

There are several degrees of Crystaline Reiki certification. The flow of energy and methods available to facilitate healing increase with each level.

Crystaline Reiki Symbols

There is a set of Crystaline Reiki symbols, as a pattern of energy, which are placed into a student's auric field during the attunements. The symbols have different uses and potentials for healing. Each higher level of Crystaline Reiki introduces more symbols for the student to use at their discretion as appropriate during a session. I will explain the healing potential for each of the Crystaline Reiki degrees and add the most likely students for that degree.

Crystaline Reiki Degree I

This is the beginner certification. The student is primarily taught the history of Crystaline Reiki and the practical hand positions to use for self-healing and healing others. There are no symbols taught at this level, so the work that can be done by a Crystaline Reiki Level I practitioner is simply the physical laying on of hands to pass the Crystaline Reiki into another. That is certainly worthwhile in and of itself by any means and can be a tremendous gift to anyone who would like to be able to channel life force energy for themselves and others.

I would suggest that anyone that is chronically or seriously ill take at least Level I Crystaline Reiki for their healing purposes, even if they never intend to work on another being. The attunement to Level I clears and balances the student's energy and will enhance the flow of vital energy that the body can hold to promote other healing functions. This is an excellent certification for anyone curious about Crystaline Reiki and who wants to enhance their vital energy but doesn't care to take on the role of a healer to other beings.

Crystaline Reiki Degree II

This is the intermediate certification. The student is taught three Crystaline Reiki symbols that serve to increase power, heal the subconscious, and "anchor in" a distant subject to perform distance healing. The distance healing ability is very handy when the person you would like to assist is not physically present. Healing prayers are a form of directed energy to assist another. Crystaline Reiki Level II allows a person to bring the intent to heal to a very magnified force and send it with precision and accuracy. I suggest this level for the serious student who has learned to utilize Crystaline Reiki Level I energy in a healing way with others. It can be used for self-healing purposes for seriously ill people, but the ability to use this level for the greater good is almost a responsibility once it's possible to assist others in this way. The attunement to Level II Crystaline Reiki clears and balances the student's emotional body and can assist in bringing up past trauma to be healed in the present. I would suggest this level for any person that feels a calling to assist others in their healing process or health care providers of any modality...especially nurses and massage therapists. Many nurses already practice therapeutic touch, and while that is different from channeling Crystaline Reiki, I believe that Crystaline Reiki can greatly enhance the effectiveness of being able to sense fluctuations in a patient's energy field and send harmonizing energy to that area. I would like to see more partnering of conventional and complementary therapies this way, and the nurses are in a particularly good position to act as the bridge between the camps.

Crystaline Reiki Degree III

The Level III practitioner is introduced to psychic surgery techniques of removing energy blocks and given another symbol during a healing session. The symbol is actually the Master symbol that serves to clear and balance the student's spiritual body, but no attempts are made to show the Level III practitioner how to teach Reiki or to pass the attunements on to others. It is specifically for the serious healer who does not care to teach Reiki to others.

Crystaline Reiki Master

This is the top of the line in Crystaline Reiki. Crystaline Reiki masters have taken this certification because they feel a passion and dedication to spread the Crystaline Reiki teachings and to assist others in becoming channels of Crystaline Reiki. Additional symbols are given that are used in the attunement process to pass the energy to another. All Crystaline Reiki masters have to go through a period of learning and are thus Crystaline Reiki masters-in-training. They have had all the possible attunements and strength of flow of a certified master but are in the process of learning how to pass on the attunements and to BE.

Crystaline Reiki Master Teacher.

I do not have to suggest this level to anyone because most Crystaline Reiki Masters immediately know it is part of their life purpose. If you need a professional Crystaline Reiki treatment, I suggest a Level II degree Crystaline Reiki practitioner. Level II and beyond can employ additional techniques to assist the client in many ways. The higher the certification, the stronger the flow of Crystaline Reiki through the practitioner and the more ways to support the healing process. The typical fees for an hour-long Crystaline Reiki session are around $50 to $60, depending on the area.

Chapter Six: Setting the Sacred Space

Setting the healing space before you begin a healing session is important. If possible, consider setting up a permanent area that can be designated as a sacred space where only spiritual things will be allowed. For the transformational healing energies to be effective, they must be established in a vortex field. The configuration on the next page will create such a space, a "Gate of Grace," if you will.

Establishing this gate creates a powerful healing space and increases the frequency and intensity of the healing process itself. This design is best laid out on the ceiling of the healing space, with the massage table or chair placed in the center of the gate and the person's head facing north. This configuration will provide the maximum energetic benefit. If one travels, the gate configuration can be laid out beneath the table, giving similar results.

Intentions

Setting a clear intention increases your ability to focus, thus assuring that the energy will flow strongly. If you are aware of your spiritual guides, this is the time to ask them for assistance. If you are not yet aware of the identity of your guides, consider asking your guardian angels to help you focus this energy. Contacting your spirit guides is explained in Chapter 8. I ask my guides, Archangel Raphael and Thoth, to assist me in the healing process. Thoth helps with the wisdom circles; he likes a crowd. You are a channel for healing energy. The energy knows where it needs to go to do the most good.

The Gate of Grace

Note	Scale	Color	Church	Stone
C	Do	Blue	Philadelphia	Blue sapphire, azurite, or blue adventurine
D	Re	Yellow	Pergamum	Yellow sapphire, yellow topaz, or yellow calcite
E	Mi	Orange	Ephesus	Orange Calcite, orange sapphire, or carnelian
F	Fa	Purple	Thyatira	Amethyst or benetoite
G	So	Red	Smyrna	Ruby Crystal or jewel
A	La	Green	Sardis	Emerald, kyanite, or fluorite
B	Ti	Violet	Laodicea	Lavender jade, violet calcite, or charoite

Let go of the outcome of the session.

As a Crystaline Reiki practitioner, you must learn to let go of the outcome of each healing session. Crystaline Reiki energy goes where it needs to go. Prime Source always has the best in mind in every situation and always works for the highest good in each healing session. Crystaline Reiki never does harm, for it is pure loving energy, simply assisting the client on his or her healing journey.

Chapter Seven: Tuning Forks in the Crystaline Reiki Process

Sound healing, in its many aspects and elements, has been a recognized modality in the healing professions for a long time, and its use is increasing rapidly. One of the areas that has seen particular growth is the use of tuning forks. Tuning forks used to clear the chakras, play a central role in Crystaline Reiki. A brief overview of the basics of using tuning forks will get you started. With practice, you will gain ease in handling the forks and see the increase in healing power they provide.

The Tuning Forks

Use: Use a soft rubber object to strike them on. We have found that a hockey puck works well. Never strike tuning forks against a hard surface or against each other; this can damage the forks and actually change their frequency. A light tap of the fork is sufficient to establish resonance. With some practice, you will see that a slight snap of the wrist works very well. Bear in mind that you may or may not be able to hear the sound of the fork, but this does not mean that it is not working. Both the rate of frequency and possible hearing damage of yourself or the patient can create the impression that the fork is not resonating properly. Unweighted forks generally resonate on a subtler plane than the weighted ones do. We have found that weighted forks seem to work better on the physical plane, whereas the un-weighted ones seem to be more effective on the astral and emotional levels.

Storage: The forks are made of aluminum and are highly sensitive instruments. Take care that the forks are not allowed to bang into each other or a foreign object. The best method of storage seems to be wrapping them separately in a soft cloth and storing them where they will not have a chance of being dropped or hit. Our experience with the use of tuning forks has fostered a great respect and admiration for the work they do, and so we have learned to treat them with great respect.

Color: The sound therapy community has assigned a color for each frequency, and each tuning fork handle is painted to correspond with the frequency of the fork. A word of caution: The paint will peel and wear off over time and use. Massage oils will accelerate the fading process, as will the natural oils from your hands. We recommend that you wash the handles of the forks after each use with warm soapy water and allow to air dry.

Various sets of forks are available. The basic set has seven tuning forks. The angelic set has four forks for the additional four chakras. The nerve fork can be added. The Genesis fork seals the healing treatment.

The correct way to hold tuning forks

Always hold only the stem handle at the bottom of the fork. Touching the prongs will stop the vibration.

Possible uses of the tuning forks in sound healing

Tone a single fork or two forks by striking the forks on a hockey puck (this does not apply to weighted forks) to create a harmonic frequency. Either hold or move (sweep) over the body or place the stem end on:

Any tissue of the body, such as bones, organs, or muscles

Acupuncture points or meridian energy lines

Reflex zones of feet, hands, ears, or head

All eleven chakras

Stem cells

Reflex points

Nerves (using the nerve fork)

Remember to use the Genesis fork after each healing session to lock into place the healing that has occurred.

Chapter Eight: Attunement Process Step One—Aligning the Chakras

The chakras

Chakra is a Sanskrit word meaning "wheel." Chakras are energy centers within the body that turn or rotate, and they process the life force energy. We are all affected by the world around us, by what we see, drink, eat, and smell, whether we are aware of it or not. Our bodies try to stay balanced twenty-four hours a day, seven days a week. Remember that disease is not a problem but rather a symptom that shows we are out of balance in some areas of our lives.

There are eleven energy centers within your body and an aura field that connects you to the twelfth, the Divine energy of source. These energy centers are connected to the organs, the meridians, and the emotional and thought centers of the body. They keep the life force energy flowing throughout the body.

Each chakra is related to a gland or several glands in the physical body. The chakras can therefore be seen as a subtle addition to the glandular system. Healing the relevant chakra will help glandular functions. Keeping the chakras in balance is an important key to good health. The chakra-clearing process will bring all eleven chakras into alignment and balance. The chakras respond to the resonance of the tuning forks and will adjust themselves to the frequency of the tuning forks. The process is simple and easy to learn. Begin with the person sitting comfortably in a chair or resting comfortably on a massage table. Instruct them to relax and just let the vibrations enter their auric field and physical body. (Always remember to set your intentions.) Tune in to the person's energies; take an overview before you begin. Call on your spirit guides and the angels to assist you, and begin.

Remember, you can use the basic tuning fork set or the basic and angelic sets with the Genesis fork.

Eleven Major Chakras

One: Start in the middle of the chakra field, which will be the fourth chakra, and move from the center to the outside. The fourth chakra, the heart chakra, corresponds to the green tuning fork. The heart chakra is the dwelling place of the soul. Strike the tuning fork on the hockey puck (or whatever you choose to use) gently and hold the fork over the heart chakra area for approximately fifteen seconds. The tuning fork should be held so that the open end of the fork, not the handle, is directed toward the patient. Be aware that the patient may or may not feel or be aware of the effects of the balancing. People are all at different levels of understanding and awareness. Not feeling anything does not mean that the process is not working. Be sure to explain that to the client, as relieving any possible anxiety is highly desirable. When the allotted time has expired, lay your tuning fork down carefully. The chakra balancing may go exactly from chakra to chakra, fifteen seconds on each one, but listen to your intuition. You may be led to repeat the tuning process more than once or to tune one chakra out of this order. Remember to follow your guidance; the tuning forks can do no harm.

Two: Now that we have the heart chakra balanced, pick up the yellow tuning fork and move down to the third chakra, which is the solar plexus area. As with the heart chakra, strike the tuning fork on the hockey puck gently and hold it over the solar plexus chakra area for approximately fifteen seconds. When finished, lay down the fork.

Three: The next chakra to be balanced is the fifth, or throat, chakra. Blue is the color associated with it. As before, carefully pick up the blue tuning fork, strike it gently, and hold it over the throat chakra area for approximately fifteen seconds. It is not uncommon for a recipient to start to feel the energy changes at this point. However, if they do not, it does not mean that something is wrong with either the patient or the healer.

Four: After the throat chakra has been balanced, put down the blue fork and pick up the orange one to balance the second chakra, located just below the navel, which is associated with the color orange. Strike the tuning fork on the hockey puck gently and hold it over the second chakra area below the navel for approximately fifteen seconds—and remember to continue to set your intent.

Five: The next chakra to be balanced is the sixth, located in the center of the forehead and commonly referred to as the third eye. The color assigned to this chakra is purple. Pick up the purple fork, strike it gently, and aim it directly at the forehead for about fifteen seconds. Be aware of the response to each tuning fork; keep your intention for healing, and follow your inner guidance as well as the client's healing guides.

Six: Next is the first chakra, more commonly called the root chakra. This is located at and right above the genitals. The tuning fork color for the root chakra is red. Pick up the red tuning fork by the handle, strike the fork gently until you get a clear vibrational tone, and hold it over the root chakra for fifteen seconds.

Seven: The last chakra located on the physical body is the seventh chakra, also known as the crown chakra. The color here is violet, and balancing is done the same way as the other six. Pick up the violet tuning fork by the handle, strike the tuning fork on the hockey puck gently, and hold it over the crown, pointing the fork six inches above the center of the head. At this point, the subject should be showing visible signs of peace, calm, and relaxation.Bear in mind that some people are so out of touch with their bodies and their real selves that they may not be able to sense anything out of the ordinary. Whether they feel it or not, the tuning forks will assist their bodies to come into balance.

At this point, we have only the four chakras outside the physical body remaining to be balanced,and the method of balancing these is slightly different. We will now use two tuning forks simultaneously for each chakra, or you can use the Angelic tuning fork set. As you have already noticed, each fork has its own vibration or sound as well as color. As any musician can tell you, when two notes are played at the same time, they create a new sound or vibration. This new "note" or "vibration" corresponds to each of the four chakras located outside the usual seven chakras.

Eight: Let's start with the Omega chakra, which requires the use of the Red and Yellow tuning forks (or the Shekinah tuning fork from the Angelic set). Hold a fork in each hand or both in one hand if you desire. Practice both ways until you discover which feels most natural for you. Strike the tuning forks until a clear tone is heard, pointing both toward the area about twelve inches below the root chakra, forming a "V" shape pointing just above the knees. Again, hold the forks for about fifteen seconds, as we have done before.

Nine: The next chakra is called the Alpha chakra and is located about twelve inches above the crown chakra. This one requires the Blue and Purple forks together. Strike the tuning forks on the hockey puck gently and hold them twelve inches above the head, pointing toward the center of the head. (You can use the Michael fork from the Angelic set.)

Ten: The terra chakra is next, and it is located in the ankle area. The tuning forks Red and Orange are used together here to energize this chakra. Strike the tuning forks on the hockey puck gently and hold them just above the ankles. (Or use the Sandalphon fork from the Angelic set.)

Eleven: The angelic chakra is the last one, and it is located twenty-four inches above the crown chakra. The Purple and the Violet forks will activate this chakra—or you can use the Metatron fork from the Angelic set—and bring the patient to the next step in the Crystaline Reiki process.

Chapter Nine: Attunement Process Step Two—Connecting with Your Spirit Guides

Now that the person or patient is balanced and aligned, we go on to the second step, connecting with your spirit guides and angels. We strongly suggest that you ask the person that you are working on to do the same with their guides. Ask your guides to connect with the guides of the person that is receiving the healing. This will help to bring clarity and precision to the process.

Place your hands, palms down, over the heart of the recipient, asking your guides to prepare the person for the increase in energy. Repeat this process on their head, asking for divine guidance to fill the person. Move to the feet and ask the guides to fully ground the person to the

Earth. Is there a place for Christians in this healing work? Absolutely! When Jesus met the Samaritan woman at the well, he told her things about herself without asking her any questions. She ran to the village to tell everyone, "This man told me everything I have ever done." This is the psychic ability. Jesus said, "Greater works than these will ye do because I go to the Father." Psychically knowing about a person's needs, sorrows, and secrets is one of those greater things. Jesus can be your guide, as well as can the angels. Take three deep breaths, and with each breath, visualize your guides sending Source energy down through the top of your head and into your heart chakra. Feel the connection of the guides as they connect with your heart chakra, sending you love from the heavens, from their dimension to yours. They will assist you in this healing/attunement process.

Remember, your guides are here to be of service to you, to bring you energy and love. Thank your guides for their assistance.

A CD is available for guided meditation for connecting to spirit guides and angels. See Resources at the end of this manual.

First, set aside the time for this powerful guided meditation. Get comfortable by sitting in a chair or sitting on the ground cross-legged. Make sure your feet are firmly planted on the floor if you are sitting, or your "sits" bones are equally grounded if you are cross-legged. Visualize your feet (or spine) being tree roots, and with each breath these roots go deeper into Mother Earth. Take a deep breath, sending down the tree roots into Mother Earth. As you exhale, feel the grounding energy of Mother Earth coming up through the bottoms of your feet, up your legs, through your hips. and into your solar plexus (3rd chakra).

Take a third deep breath, and this time send your tree roots down into the very center of Mother Earth, into her crystal core, and locking into the center of this crystal core, anchoring your very self into its grounding energy.

Now that you are fully grounded, let us move on to the next step in this meditative process.

Call your spirit guides by name, and ask them to send you their angelic energies. Take a deep breath and feel the energies of the guides as they send their energies down through the crown of the head (crown chakra) to the center of the chest (heart chakra). Take a second deep breath, again bringing your spirit guide's energies down through the crown of the head and into the center of your being, the hcart chakra.

Chapter Ten: Attunement Process Step Three—Transmission of the Crystaline Reiki Symbol

The person is now balanced, aligned, and connected to their spirit guides. They are ready to receive the transmission of the symbol of Crystaline Reiki. This symbol is passed on to the person only if they are being attuned to the status of Crystaline Reiki Master Teacher.

You can also use this symbol when doing healing work on this person. If the person is sitting, stand behind them. If they are lying down, then position yourself at their head. Placing your hands on their head, draw the symbol on their crown chakra. Now draw the symbol on each shoulder, and with your hands still on their shoulders, allow the energy to flow into them for a few minutes.

When you sense that they have received an ample amount, then move to their third eye and draw the symbol three times while visualizing the symbol embedding itself on their intuitive center. This will open the person's third eye to greater intuitive vision.

Proceed to the heart chakra and repeat the process. Do the same with each foot, fully grounding it into the person.

Chapter Eleven: Attunement Process—The Final Step

If you are attuning someone to the status of Crystaline Reiki Master Teacher, there is a little more to do. Otherwise, use the Genesis tuning fork and close the session. Close the session by following: Tap the Genesis fork and wave the fork over the entire body from head to toe three times, outlining figure eight (the infinity sign). This process "sets" the energy in place. Advise the recipient to rest on the table for five to fifteen minutes before getting up, ensuring they have water available when they rise, as this process can dehydrate a person very quickly.

If you are attuning someone to the Crystaline Reiki method, this is a great time to discuss the process they just went through, what they felt, how they feel now, and what they plan on doing with this new energy. Set up a time with them for a session where they will do the Crystaline Reiki work on you. This will allow you to ensure they have received the transfer of energy, for you will certainly sense it if they have. You may also use this time to teach them how to transfer energy to another person, as well as the proper methods for doing a healing session. Be sure to give them their certificate of completion for the level of attunement that they have just received.

Chapter Twelve: Meditations

I share these processes with you in the hope that your adventures into this aspect of our consciousness will be as exciting as mine have been. To begin with, accept the subtle energies of the world around you as reality. These energies play as vital a role as human beings do in planetary evolution. Recognize the life force in everything you see, smell, touch, taste, and hear, as well as in what you cannot sense or imagine. Accepting their reality and capacity to interact with you intelligently is a necessary part of this work. Listen and honor the directions of your inner voice system or intuition. Follow the directions of intuition by closely listening to your true feelings. Do not write them off as imagination. With experience, you will learn to distinguish the fact that imagination and logic come from the left brain, and intuition, with its base in feelings, flows from the right brain. Intuition simply informs without analysis or judgment. Remember, it is the voice of your true self, so learn to trust it. Develop your third eye vision by strengthening the third eye chakra, which lies in the center of your forehead directly above the beginning of your eyebrows. There are a number of yogic and non-yogic exercises that can help you do this.

Spend time alone amidst nature. Use all five senses to establish a close rapport with the wonders of creation. Kinesthetically feel the places and persons you meet routinely. Get familiar with your energy, and develop the habit of feeling the vibrations around you. Using your kinesthetic sense is an important part of all energy work.

Love Light meditation

Complete the Love Light meditation before attempting to tune into another's energy field. With your eyes closed, feel your love spread through the whole universe. Establish in your mind that you are a divine being, and then use your third eye to visualize your subject with complete love and respect. Request permission from his higher self to make this connection. Listen carefully, as your intuition will translate the answer to you. To scan your subject (this step is a continuation of fine-tuning), continue to focus on your third eye center. Empty your mind of all biases and judgments. Become thought-free using your inner vision. Scan your subject's physical body slowly from head to toe. Repeat this exercise three times. Again, remember what you "see." Scan the first three layers of the aura one by one. Do this three times. Again, remember what you see. Ask your subject's higher self if it has any information for you. Wait for a response.

End this meditation by thanking yourself, your subject, his higher self, and all the divine energies that made this connection possible. Note down all the details of the fine-tuning and scanning. This information is privileged and should not be conveyed to anyone except the person concerned or his representative.

Crystaline Reiki meditation

This meditation can bring about relaxation, clairvoyance, increased healing ability, enhanced awareness, greater ability toward visualization, balanced energy, and assistance in reaching your goals.

1. Sit comfortably, either with legs folded on a cushion or on a straight-back chair. Keep your spine erect (without force). If you are sitting on a chair, do not lean back. Rub your hands together and place them on your knees or in another place comfortable for you.

2. Relax and breathe slowly; think about Crystaline Reiki; ask your Reiki and spirit guides to join you.

3. Draw the Crystaline master symbol in front of you with your whole hand. Visualize how a white or violet light comes out through your fingers as you draw the symbol in the air in front of you.

4. Visualize the symbol in the third eye chakra and recite its name three times. Keep the symbol steadily in your third eye.

5. When you feel you have meditated enough on this symbol, let it float into a field of light above your head. Return your consciousness to the third eye chakra.

6. Repeat steps 3 to 5 with the mental/emotional symbol and the distance symbol used in the Usui method.

7. When you are finished meditating on the three symbols, you will be concentrated and full of healing Crystaline Reiki energy. You can now continue with the final part of the meditation, where you can send Crystaline Reiki to your projects and goals or heal others at a distance.

8. Send Crystaline Reiki by visualizing or describing the object, goals, or person. You can use the method you have learned or the one you feel most suits you.

9. When finished, slowly relax and release all thoughts. Sit quietly for a few minutes and enjoy the peace.

10. Rub your hands together and "wash" your face with them. Open your eyes, walk a few steps, and feel how refreshed you are. Thank your Crystaline Reiki and spirit guides for their assistance in this meditation process.

Crystaline Light Meditation

Spend ten minutes daily on the love light meditation to dramatically alter the quality of your day.

1. Focus on each part of the body. Starting from the feet, progressively relax each part consciously until you reach the crown of the head.

2. Repeat the last step by breathing love and gratitude in every part of your body. Give special attention to stiff or painful areas. Thank your higher self.

Close your eyes, go into your mind, and imagine a ball of white light hovering six inches above your head (your crown chakra). See this white light as bright, clear, and filled with the most wonderful energy you have ever experienced.

5. Feel the energy from this ball as it floats above your head. Focus on your crown chakra area and allow it to open to receive the energy from this ball of white light.

6. As you open your crown chakra to receive this energy, you feel completely at ease, completely safe.

7. Draw down this light energy into your forehead, eyes, nose, cheeks, and chin.

8. Draw down this white light energy into your throat, shoulders, elbows, wrists, to every finger. Feel the energy in your fingertips right now; feel them tingle with energy and excitement.

9. Draw the white light energy down your chest, hips, thighs, knees, calves, and ankles into every toe. Feel the toes tingle as the energy fills them. Picture this white light energy filling up your entire body. Now, expand this white light energy to include your house and breathe love into it. Expand your love to all the people who are a part of your life. Spread your love for the city you live in. Reach with love towards your country and then the whole world. Include mountains, cities, rivers, and humanity in general.

15. Feel the floor of love energy from your heart engulfing the world and the whole universe.

Maintain the feeling of love for a few minutes. Withdraw your aura back towards your body. Thank yourself and God for this beautiful experience.

Grounding Meditation

Used when you have that "spaced out" feeling. Helps to focus one's attention on the here and now. Begin by taking a deep, slow breath in;

release slowly out. Do several times, paying attention to your body responding by allowing stress and tensions to flow out and away. Close your eyes and picture yourself as your favorite tree. Feel roots sprouting from the soles of your feet and going deeper...deeper into Mother Earth to the very center of her core. Feel strong, feel rooted, and feel grounded. When you can feel the strength that comes from being fully grounded in Mother Earth, move your thoughts up your legs, torso, shoulders, neck, and face to the top of your head. Feel branches sprouting from the top of your head, reaching...stretching...opening towards Father Sky. Higher, higher, towards Father Sky. Feel the great expansion from your branches. Bring your thoughts back to your roots and slowly inhale the energy that is freely given to you from Mother Earth. Inhale slowly up the trunk of your body and exhale through the branches over your head.

Feel the cycle of breath energy coming up from your roots and showering over your head through the branches. Continue for a few more breaths. When you are ready, open your eyes. Feel stronger. Feel grounded. Another technique that may help you feel grounded is removing your shoes and allowing your bare feet to play in the dirt. Wiggling your toes in the sand at the beach may also be wiggling your toes in the sand at the beach. When I had trouble grounding myself, I would go to the beach, dig two holes, stick my feet in them, and cover them with sand. I would then begin my grounding meditations. You can also hold a handful of fresh dirt in your hands, and feel the energy in the soil. Contemplate it, exchange with it. You may bring it into the house and place it in a bowl to bring your focus to the earth, thus grounding it.

You can also wear articles of clothing that are black, brown, or other earth tones to help you with the feeling of groundedness. Wearing a talisman or meditating with some of the following crystals/gemstones may also help hematite, onyx, black tourmaline, aurauralite, or tiger's eye.

Chapter Thirteen: Choosing A Crystaline Reiki Teacher

People living in the Spokane and Coeur d'Alene areas are blessed with many choices of Reiki instructors. There truly is someone for everyone. The wealth of choices, however, can sometimes make it more difficult to compare the differences and make a wise decision. Following are some tips that may help you choose someone appropriate for you.

Compatibility

Sharing energy is very personal. Above all else, energetic compatibility is key to your class experience. Don't be timid. Ask questions, listen with your "inner ear," and honor the intuition or feelings you get as a prospective teacher speaks with you. If you feel good about a person and their philosophies, your experience likely will be positive as well. If you aren't sure, consider getting a Reiki session from a couple of prospective teachers you feel most drawn to. This will allow you to share their energy and demeanor, experience how they work, and view their practice environment.

Honoring You

Reiki is about sharing energy from the heart and the honoring of all individuals as they are in each moment. Although Reiki practitioners and teachers deserve to make a living, Reiki is not primarily about business, and it is not about competition. Your teacher should honor and respect you at all times, be grateful to support you and the growth of your practice, act with honesty and integrity, and always work to support your best interests.

Practice Experience

Ask prospective teachers about their practitioner experience. It is easy to obtain a Master Teacher certificate within a very short time. However, it takes time, consistent practice, and ongoing personal growth work to develop awareness, understanding, and application of the Reiki principles to daily life. Suppose someone last used Reiki in practice a considerable time before teaching. In that case, they are less likely to develop the awareness, understanding, and range of practical experience needed to meet the responsibilities of an instructor.

Philosophy

The practice of Reiki has evolved considerably over the years and has and will continue to do so. There are many variations in its practice and teaching. These range from the traditional Usui foundational base to newer forms that continue to be introduced. Usui Reiki provides the core foundation from which you can grow and expand. This typically is required before other forms of Reiki are taken. Teachers may have different philosophies about what Reiki "is" and how it "should" be used. Some are rigidly traditional, while others may diverge to the point that the traditional foundation is lost. A good guideline is to look for someone who respects others' ways but at the same time provides balanced approaches and offers courses that will give you a good basic foundation from which to begin. Ask a prospective teacher about their philosophies and approaches to Reiki and choose someone whose responses feel compatible with what feels "right" for you.

Investment

There now appears to be a wider variety of fees for Reiki classes than in the past. Just as fees may vary, there also may be considerable differences in quality and in what you receive for your investment. Therefore, it is wise to consider your purpose for taking this training, both now and in the future. If you have the desire to begin a formal Reiki practice, to integrate it with other work you do, or to use it on others apart from yourself and your family, consider the value of finding a high-quality, comprehensive class that will provide you with certification and the tools, information, and deeper understanding you will need to offer public service.Following are some factors you may want to consider in relation to your needs and circumstances:

Reiki Materials

Reiki class materials may range from a few photocopied handouts to full manuals. Sometimes a full manual may be included in your registration cost, or you may be asked to pay extra for one. Ask about this and understand what exactly you are getting. Good reference materials will be important to you later as you integrate and practice what you learned in class.

Class Length

Individual classes may range from a few hours to two days. Especially in Level 1 and Master Teacher, if a class is less than a full day, time will force you to sacrifice either foundational background or valuable hands-on practice time. Note if someone charges you nearly as much for a half-day class as others do for a full day or more. Be particularly wary if someone offers two levels on a single day. Practice time. Reiki is experiential and can be learned and integrated only through adequate practice. Find out approximately how much time in each level is spent on bookwork or lecture vs. experiential activities. You need time to understand the background, foundation, philosophy, and feeling and experience of using Reiki. I feel that the average ratio should be approximately 50 percent experiential for Level 1 and at least 75 percent experiential for Levels 2 and above.

Student Support

It is typical for questions or issues to arise after you have left class and begun to practice Reiki and process your attunement. Your teacher should be there to freely support you after you leave class. Will your teacher be easily accessible to you, and in what ways and to what extent? Will she/he promptly respond to you when you need it?

Continuing Education Requirements

If you need your Reiki class to meet the requirements for continuing professional education, verify that your prospective teacher is currently approved by the appropriate licensing agency to offer the credit hours you need. A teacher's class advertisements should specify their credentials, the type of CE they are approved to offer, and the number of hours they will receive. If this needs to be clarified, be sure to ask. If in doubt, call your licensing board to verify.

Organization

Your prospective Reiki teacher should be able and willing to provide you with at least the following before you register: clear written information about what is included in each class; fees and policies on cancellations and refunds; any preparation required on your part; and class time and class location. You also should receive reasonably prompt confirmation of your place in the class and of receipt of your payments.

Chapter Fourteen: Training Crystaline Reiki

Crystalline Reiki is a divine gift from the spirit that benefits everyone regardless of their spiritual path or beliefs. It is my intent to pass the energy of Crystalline Reiki on to as many people as possible, and learning Crystaline Reiki is now available in great new ways. Because of the time constraints of our busy lives, we don't always have time to sit in an eight- or sixteen-hour class. I am guided to offer the Crystaline Reiki attunement in new ways.

In-Person

Classes are scheduled regularly at The Family of Light Healing Center in Spokane, Washington, and in Devon, England. Classes are not only the most traditional way to learn Crystaline Reiki but are a great interactive way to learn, practice, and get feedback from others in your area. I am always available for questions and feedback after your training, and I will try to provide an opportunity to practice with a Crystaline Reiki group following the training. And it's always a fun, lighthearted class!

Apprentice/One-On-One Training

We meet for a few hours to do regular training, but doing it one-on-one allows for great customization and personalized feedback. I can teach you exactly what you need to know and skip the stuff you already know (such as chakras and what energy is—but only if you want to skip it!) A two-hour (or less/more, depending on need) training includes a personal attunement, a certification of completion, and practice time. One does need to be an apprentice to use this method successfully. To learn more about my apprentice program, visit the website: www.thefamilyoflight.com

Correspondence Course

The Crystaline Reiki Correspondence Course is an advanced course for all Reiki therapists, Reiki healers, and shamanic healers. The tuition fee is $150 for the complete course.

At the end of the final examination, you will receive a diploma certified by The Family of Light Healing Center. At this time, you will also receive your final attunements, which will confirm your right to the status of Crystaline Reiki Master.

Reading Material

Immediately upon your enrollment, new students receive a copy of this book as well as lists of recommended books, crystals, gemstones, and tuning forks. I am happy to answer questions if you have them.

No Time Limits!

All students work at their own pace, in their own time to meet the needs of their own domestic and professional commitments. You may take as long as you wish to complete reading and studying the material.

Written Examination

A one-hour written examination is taken in your own home at the completion of the course material. Students achieving 70 percent are awarded the title of Crystaline Reiki Master. After completing your written examination, you will receive the final attunements to confirm your new status as Crystaline Reiki Master.

Online/Distance Training

This is a popular, growing choice. It is my belief that Crystaline Reiki healing done at a distance is very powerful, so why can't training and attunements be done at a distance? No need to seek out a teacher in person, which is helpful if you live in a remote area. This training is designed for people who learn well on their own, utilizing a variety of resources such as books and online information. How does a distance attunement happen? A time is set up for us to work together energetically from our own locations. We hold the space for you to receive the attunement, and I do the attunement over "etheric mail" as if you were sitting right in front of me. Intent is everything, so if you are ready and willing to receive the energy of Crystaline Reiki, you will. Your training includes a distance attunement, and my Crystaline Reiki manual will be purchased either as an e-book or paper copy sent by mail, and any questions you may have will be answered by email. We can schedule time for you to learn and understand Crystaline Reiki and its dynamic healing energy process.

Following the attunement, I will send your certificate either by email or mail. I am happy to answer questions and offer guidance by email following the training. You may make payments by check or PayPal (on the Family of Light website: www.thefamilyoflight.com).

Chapter Fifteen: Preparing To Teach a Crystaline Reiki Class

While a Crystaline Reiki master teacher class will provide the basic tools to become a successful Crystaline Reiki instructor, no one is fully prepared to teach immediately. Preparing for a quality class involves thought, inner guidance, preparation, and, often, personal growth work in the interim. There is no "correct" time frame, however, in which to wait and prepare. Each individual must follow his/her own guidance and sense of integrity and purpose. As the inner guiding light of our life purpose, the universal energy usually has a way of providing us with fairly clear signals of when it is our time to begin. This often occurs by people approaching us and requesting training before we have formally offered a class. When the teacher is ready, the students will begin to appear. This may come to us as a surprise, or it may follow soon after we begin to intuitively sense that the time is approaching. The universe also has a way of taking care of us. If we prepare and advertise a class before we are fully ready, it is most likely that the class will simply not draw participants. This does not mean that we made a "mistake." It is more likely that the time is getting near, and we were being put "on notice" to begin preparing and to learn something from this experience.

Gain Practice Experience

Although we certainly will continue to learn for as long as we teach, I feel very strongly that we should gain considerable experience in reading the energy body and practicing Crystaline Reiki on many different subjects before we attempt to teach it. It is easy to repeat the philosophy, historical background, and theories we were taught, but our students deserve and will gain the most from a teacher who can share a range of first-hand personal experiences. You will energetically attract the students who are most compatible with your particular teaching style and abilities and whose spiritual essences most resonate with your particular gifts and experiences. Giving yourself time to develop and know your strengths and gifts, and to better understand your challenges, will increase your confidence and guide you in the best way to structure and promote your classes.

Compatibility and Timing

Sharing energy is very personal, and compatibility is key to a positive class experience for everyone. Expect prospective students to ask questions about your background, training, experience, and philosophies. Some may want to meet you or to receive a session from you prior to choosing your class.Don't be offended or take it personally if a prospect decides he/she would rather study with someone else or if someone takes one class from you and other class levels elsewhere. Many factors contribute to a student's choices that often bear no reflection on your abilities or competence or the quality of your classes. Help empower others by encouraging prospective Reiki students to honor their intuition, feelings, and preferences. No one of us is here to serve everyone, and there are enough appropriate students for all teachers. If someone needs something you cannot provide, be open and willing to refer that person to someone else if possible. If you sincerely have a desire to serve beyond the sight range own immediate tangible benefit, you will receive an abundance far exceeding the registration fee of that student. Honor your own guidance in assisting prospective students with choosing classes. Those in your group who are just beginning to learn about energy or spiritual development may need your guidance to better understand what is involved, what a class may be like, or to choose the time frame for their classes. Be patient and compassionate and assist them to the best of your ability. If you strongly sense that someone would best be served by slowing their pace or that they would benefit from some healing or personal growth work prior to taking a class, it is appropriate to provide this kind of information for them to consider in making their choices.

Honor Your Students and Other Teachers

Crystaline Reiki is about sharing energy from the heart and fully respecting all individuals as they are in the moment. It is imperative that you respect your students at all times and that you provide an emotionally (as well as physically) safe environment for them to learn and expand. Remember that when you are teaching, your students look to you as a mentor and example of what it means to live the Crystaline Reiki principles. Honor your students and be one with them, knowing that they also are there for you in as meaningful a way as you are there for them. The questions, experiences, and energy they bring to the classroom also teach you. Be sensitive to each person's personal boundaries, feelings, and needs. Encourage them, positively focus on their personal gifts, and guide them gently and lovingly in how to expand and strengthen their abilities. Also, serve as an example of the spirit of Oneness by showing respect for all Reiki lineages, forms, and teachers. Refrain from being drawn into discussions that promote judgment or criticism of other instructors. If someone poses a question or comment based on an unpleasant experience they had with another teacher or practitioner, use this opportunity to illustrate positively how to handle things through the true spirit of Reiki.

Organizing your classes

Before you teach your first class, you will have several decisions and preparations to make, for example, How will you charge? What materials will you use? What will you include? Where will you teach, and how often? How will you attract students?

Materials and Content

I have seen Reiki class materials ranging from photocopied handouts to full manuals. Some teachers prefer to develop their own manuals, while some purchase materials for their students from other teachers or organizations such as the International Center for Reiki Training or the International Association of Reiki Professionals. Your choice in this may be influenced by your ability to write and organize information as well as what information you feel is important to include in your classes. Whatever your choices, keep in mind that good reference materials will be important to your students as they begin to practice and integrate what they learned in class. If you choose to create your own manual, know to the best of your ability the sources of your materials and be aware of your responsibilities regarding copyright laws.

Class length

I have seen individual class levels listed with ranges from four hours to three days. You will have to decide what feels most appropriate in relation to your content and teaching strategies. Experiment and continue to refine things after you have an opportunity to see how your plan works in practical application. Prepare an outline with key points and a logical flow of information and exercises, but during class, stay in the moment, be flexible, and let your inner guidance direct you. Feel free to stick to a flexible time schedule. Let the Crystaline Reiki energy and a connection with the energy of your students flow through you and guide you just as you would do in a therapeutic session. No two classes are ever the same. The more you can flow with your respective students' characteristics, needs, and experiences, the more genuine and meaningful your classes will be. Keep in mind that Crystaline Reiki is experiential and can only learn and integrated through good practice. Your students need time to understand the bookwork (background, foundation, and philosophy) of Crystaline Reiki as well as the feeling and experience of using it. I feel that the average ratio should be at least 50 percent experiential for Level 1 and at least 75 percent experiential for Levels 2 and 3.

Fees

How a teacher chooses to charge for Crystaline Reiki instruction is very individual. Many new teachers initially struggle with this, and you must follow your own inner guidance in deciding what feels right for you. There is a fairly standard fee range among professionals who have chosen therapeutic practice and teaching as their primary source of livelihood. Information on the general range for your locale can be obtained by looking at the ads or websites of other teachers in your area and by talking with others in your Reiki community. There are those who choose to charge less than the standard or to provide more opportunities for low-income individuals. There also are some who strongly believe that Crystaline Reiki and its training should be offered on a love-offering basis. I feel that there is no right or wrong position. You must make your own choices in relation to your personal needs and desires. As you choose, you must primarily consider the degree to which you are making your decisions from a state of inner balance in body, mind, and spirit.

Student Support

It will be common for your students to have questions or issues arise after they have completed your class. You should be available to support and encourage them within reasonable bounds as they integrate and practice what they have learned.

General management

How you deal with prospective students who inquire about your classes and how you deal with them during and after class can greatly contribute to building your reputation as a Crystaline Reiki teacher in your community. Practitioners and master teachers are responsible for representing Crystaline Reiki honestly and professionally at all times. Brochures, flyers, and promotional materials should not sensationalize, make misleading claims or guarantees, or make derogatory implications toward other lineages or practices. When promoting classes and services, it is your responsibility to provide enough information about your content, materials, philosophies, fees, and professional qualifications for prospective students and clients to make informed choices. At the minimum, the following information should be made available to prospective students:

Clear written information about the content of each class

Full disclosure regarding all fees and what they include

Policies on cancellations and refunds

The length of class time

If applicable, prompt confirmation of their place in the class and of your receipt of their payment

If you collect deposits with a final balance due, include in your confirmation a statement of the amount received, the amount due, and when it is due.

Anticipate your students' needs and make sure they are provided with written information on the time and location of the class and anything they should know or do to be prepared for the day of class.

Also, let them know how they can reach you the night before and on the morning of class if necessary. Do not assume that they will have this from a previous source, such as a promotional flyer. Please include it in your confirmation of their registration. It also is a good idea to specifically ask each student how he or she would like their name printed on their Crystaline Reiki certificate. Some people, particularly those in professional practices, like to include a middle initial or full name that may need to be reflected in how they provide their name for registration purposes.

In Summary

Teaching Crystaline Reiki is a deeply rewarding experience and greatly adds to health improvement and human consciousness on the planet. If you have been getting the sense that it is time to teach but have hesitated out of fear or lack of confidence, use Crystaline Reiki to help you overcome those issues and begin. You will be glad you did.

Afterword

Now that you have read the Crystaline Reiki manual, it's time to decide if this form of healing is right for you. Learning Crystaline Reiki is easy if you have the willingness to learn. Open your heart and receive the activation of the natural healer that is inside each of you. I learn something new every day, especially from my Crystal/ Indigo daughter. Make a choice to learn more about Crystaline Reiki, sound healing, progressive healing, vibrational yoga, Metis Shamanism, Sacred Stone healing, Spiritual healing, or any of the other classes or workshops available here at the Family of Light Healing Centre. Please contact me at charleslightwalker@yahoo.com and visit our website at http://www.thefamilyoflight.com/.

I trust you have enjoyed reading about Crystaline Reiki. You are blessed...

Charles Lightwalker

Resources

Books:

Creative Visualization by Shakti Gawain Essential Reiki by Diane Stein

Heal Your Body by Louise L. Hay

Modern Reiki–Method for Healing by Hiroshi Doi

Rainbow Medicine by Wolf Moondance

Reiki for Beginners by David F. Vennells

Teachings of the Masters by Dr. Joseph Crane

When You Reach the End of Your Rope, LET GO! by Geoffrey Rose, Ph.D.

Other books by Charles Lightwalker:

Vibrational Yoga: Sonic Mysticism and Movement Medical Intuition Handbook

Sound Healing with Tuning Forks

Tuning Forks:

Standard chakra set (7 forks) $175

Tree of Life tuning forks $275

Set of four Angel forks $135

Set of seven Solfeggio forks $195

Sefirot tuning forks $275

Genesis frequency $45

50 Hz nerve fork $75

The 03-zone fork $85

The psychic forks set for $295

Energy tuning fork $60

Fat burner tuning fork $110

Circulation fork $45

The Use of Tuning Forks in Vibratory Energy Application, by Diane Hesse, is the best book I have found on this subject. It covers all facets of tuning forks in the healing process.

Cost:$35, plus shipping

Gate of Grace: Sacred Healing Space

This set of eight stones is used to create a sacred healing space or open an angelic gateway used for healing and for angelic communication. All the instructions for putting it together are included.

Small gate sets: $25, plus shipping

Crystaline Reiki Meditation CD $10, includes shipping

www.thefamilyoflight.com

Seven Levels of Certification in Sound Healing With Tuning Forks

Level I - The Practitioner level offers training in the Sound Healing Chakra Balancing Technique, Nerve Fork use, Energy Fork use, and more. Four hours of instruction and hands-on experience!

Level II –Crystaline Reiki Master training. The use of tuning forks in the Reiki process includes a copy of the book Crystaline Reiki: A New Frequency of Healing.

Level III – The Meridian Therapy Process. How to use various tuning forks on the Meridians to create overall health and well-being.

Level IV-Emotional Balancing/Emotional Release. This class uses the tuning forks along with the Intuitive Emotional Release Technique to allow the client to release emotional blockages.

Level V- Organs and Glands consist of a hands-on approach to using the tuning forks on the Organs and Glands to create health.

Level VI- Advanced Practitioner Training, consists of more hands-on time, a deeper understanding of the history and theory, and training in the Chakra Balancing Technique, Intuitive Emotional Release Technique, Crystaline Reiki, and Opening the Psychic Pathways, using various Tuning Forks.

Level VII- The Teacher Certification Level certifies you to hold your own workshops within the established The Family of Light Healing Centre guidelines and discounted pricing on Tuning Forks and Training Materials.

Workshops are usually held on Saturday, and various Workshop Packages are available--some of which also include a set of the Solfeggio Tuning Forks at substantial savings. All workshop prices include a copy of the book *Sound Healing with Tuning Forks* by Charles Lightwalker.

9 781916 770478